THE BIG EASY FLOWERS
LARGE PRINT COLORING BOOK

H.R. Wallace Publishing

Copyright © 2023 by H.R. Wallace. All rights reserved. No part of this book may be reproduced or transmitted in any form or by any means whatsoever without written permission from the publisher.

Every effort has been made to ensure that this book is complete and accurate. However, no responsibility is assumed for any human error, typographical mistakes, or any consequences resulting from the use of this book. The material in this book is provided "as is" without warranty of any kind.

Images used under license from Shutterstock.com

ISBN-10: 1-5091-0266-3
ISBN-13: 978-1-5091-0266-2

www.ingramcontent.com/pod-product-compliance
Lightning Source LLC
Chambersburg PA
CBHW080939040426
42444CB00030B/3416